SIMPLE PUPPETS

from Everyday Materials

Barbara MacDonald Buetter

Sterling Publishing Co., Inc. New York
A STERLING/TAMOS BOOK

For Alicia and Justin – BMB

A Sterling/Tamos Book

10 9 8 7 6 5 4 3 2 1

First paperback edition published in 1998 by
Sterling Publishing Company, Inc.
387 Park Avenue South, New York, N.Y. 10016

Tamos Books Inc.
300 Wales Avenue, Winnipeg, MB, Canada R2M 2S9

© 1996 by Barbara MacDonald Buetter
Illustrations © by Barbara MacDonald Buetter and George Buetter

Design   Barbara MacDonald Buetter and George Buetter
Photography   Custom Images Ltd.

Distributed in Canada by Sterling Publishing
℅ Canadian Manda Group, One Atlantic Avenue, Suite 105
Toronto, Ontario, Canada M6K 3E7
Distributed in Great Britain and Europe by Cassell PLC
Wellington House, 125 Strand, London WC2R 0BB, England
Distributed in Australia by Capricorn Link (Australia) Pty Ltd.
P.O. Box 6651, Baulkham Hills, Business Centre, NSW 2153, Australia
Printed in China
All rights reserved

Canadian Cataloging-in-Publication Data
MacDonald Buetter, Barbara
     Simple Puppets
     "A Sterling/Tamos book."
     Includes Index.
     ISBN 1-895569-05-2
1.   Puppet making–Juvenile literature.
I.   Title.
TT174.7.M34 1996   j745.592'24   C95–920258–7

Library of Congress Cataloging-in-Publication Data
Buetter, Barbara Macdonald.
     Simple puppets with everyday materials / Barbara
MacDonald Buetter.
          p.   cm.
     " Sterling/Tamos Book."
     Includes Index.
     Summary: Provides directions for making all kinds of
puppets out of easily obtainable materials, including socks, paper
rolls, boxes, spools, and even vegetables.
     ISBN 1-895569-05-2
     1.   Puppet making--Juvenile literature.   [1. Puppet
making. 2. Handicraft.]   I. Title.
TT174.7.B84   1996   96-15475
745.592'24--dc20   CIP
                                             AC

Sterling ISBN 1-895569-05-2 Trade
               1-895569-35-4 Paper

TABLE OF CONTENTS

Puppets are for Everyone!

Do you like pretending? You can make your favorite imaginary characters come alive with puppets. This book will show you how to make simple puppets and use them to act out your own stories.

Making puppets is fun and easy if you follow some basic instructions. And don't be afraid to try different things, to use your own ideas. The projects in this book will get you started, and before you know it your imagination will take over and you'll be creating your own designs. That's where the fun really starts!

With each puppet is a list of supplies and simple instructions. Many of the things you'll need can be found around the house. If you do want to buy supplies, most can be found at your local hobby or craft shop.

It's a good idea to save an empty box and use it to store your own collection of recycled craft supplies–toilet rolls, old socks, anything that you think you might use.

Most of the puppets will need painting or gluing, so be sure to cover your work surface before starting, and pick a spot that can be easily washed up.

There's no special order, so look through all the projects before you decide which one to try first. You'll have fun making these characters and that's just the beginning. Your puppet plays are sure to be great if the stars of the show are your own special puppets!

Recycled Supplies

Your collection of recycled materials may give you ideas for unusual puppet decorations. Here are some of the things you might save from around your house.

Popsicle sticks	Cotton balls
Pop tabs	Buttons and beads
Lids from plastic containers	Straws
Felt and fabric scraps	Feathers
Paper towel/toilet tissue tubes	Thread, string, or yarn
Egg cartons	Wrapping paper
	Magazines and newspapers
	Old mitts

Flattened cereal boxes provide lightweight cardboard.

Plastic bags can be shredded and glued on for hair.

Chenille stems can be shaped into glasses, whiskers, or antennae.

Eggshells can be washed and crushed between two plates, to glue on as sparkles.

Before you start each project, gather all the supplies you'll need and any extras you might use.

Here's a Tip

If the directions call for tacky or fabric glue, don't substitute regular craft glue. The tacky glue is thicker and stronger, and is perfect for hard-to-stick things such as fabric, tin foil, or plastic.

Basic Decorating Techniques

Many of the puppets in this book have glued-on arms, legs, faces, and decorations.
Here are some basic techniques you can use to make these added features.
You'll find other decorating ideas as you read through the projects in this book.

PAPER CHAINS

1 Cut colored paper into short strips. Use different colors if you like.

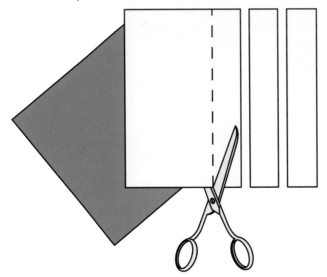

2 Roll one strip into a circle and glue the ends together.

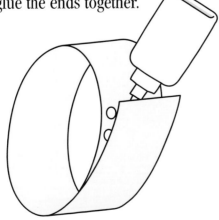

3 Insert a second strip through the middle of the first, then roll it into a circle and glue the ends together.

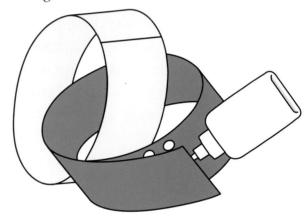

4 Continue adding links to your paper chain until it's the right length.

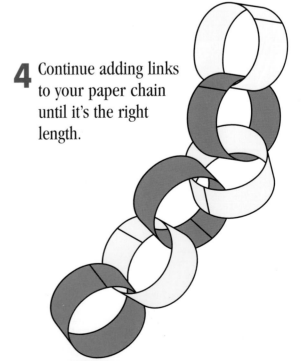

BRAIDING

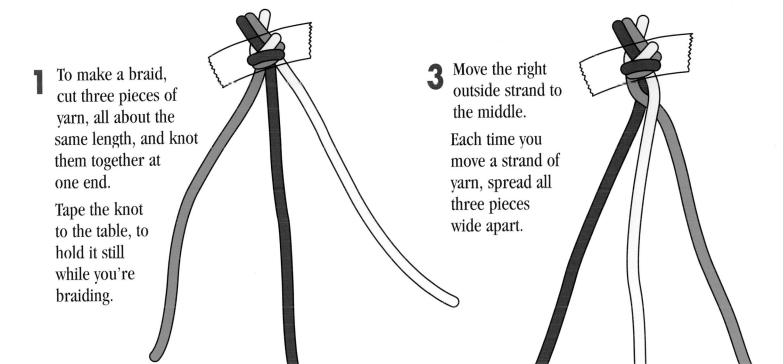

1 To make a braid, cut three pieces of yarn, all about the same length, and knot them together at one end.

Tape the knot to the table, to hold it still while you're braiding.

2 Move the left outside strand to the middle.

Spread the three pieces of yarn apart again.

3 Move the right outside strand to the middle.

Each time you move a strand of yarn, spread all three pieces wide apart.

4 Continue moving outside strands to the middle, changing sides each time.

You're braiding!

Keep going until you near the end of the yarn. Then knot the ends together or wind an elastic band tight around them.

9

THREE-DIMENSIONAL PARTS

NOSES

1 For a three-dimensional nose, fold a paper triangle in half.

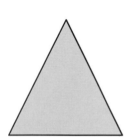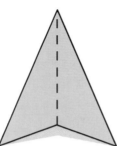

2 Turn the folded triangle over and make another fold along each flat edge, folding in towards the middle.

Put glue on these two side tabs and glue the nose in place on the puppet.

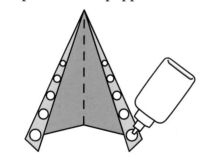

EARS

1 For ears that stick out, cut out two small construction paper ovals and fold each one in half.

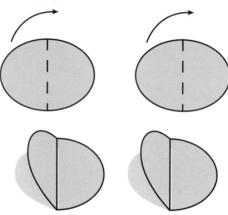

2 For each ear, put glue on the back of one half and press the glued half onto the puppet in position.

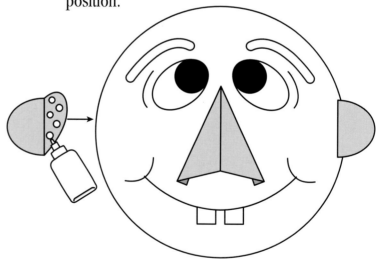

Use this folded paper technique for three-dimensional noses, ears, beaks, arms, wings, or tails. Cut out the shapes you want, with extra tabs to fold back, and glue them onto the puppet.

10

HATS

CROWNS

1 For a crown, cut a paper rectangle just long enough to wrap all around your puppet's head. Draw the points of the crown along one long edge, then cut them out.

2 Use paints or markers to add decorations, or glue on paper cutouts.

3 Roll the crown into a circle and use glue or clear tape to join the edges.

CONE HATS

1 To make a cone-shaped hat, cut out a paper circle about twice as big as your puppet's head. Cut in from the edge of the circle to the center.

2 Overlap the cut edges of the circle until the cone is the right shape. Then tape the edge down in position.

Decorate the hat with paper cutouts or markers.

3 To keep the hat on, put dots of glue around the bottom of the cone, along the inside. Then press the hat onto the puppet's head.

11

Happy

Making Faces

Your puppet's face tells the audience a lot about its character or about how it's "feeling". The eyes, the mouth, even the curve of the eyebrows can change the expression. Practice drawing the faces shown here, then create some of your own. Make faces in the mirror and copy the shape of your mouth and your eyebrows. Use big, exaggerated features–the more outrageous, the better.

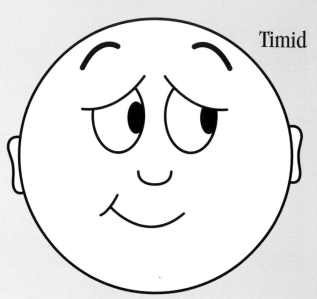
Timid

Grumpy

Worried

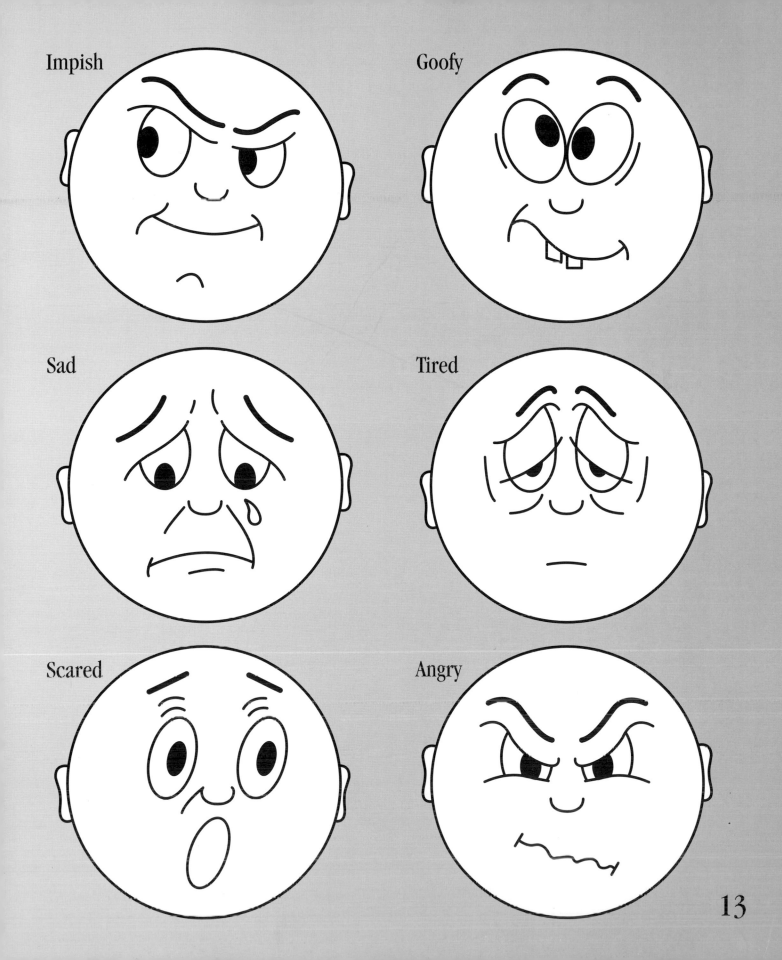

Impish

Goofy

Sad

Tired

Scared

Angry

13

Walking Puppet

Once you've practiced drawing different faces, choose your favorite and make a mask. With this paper plate mask, you can join the show as a "walking puppet!"

SUPPLIES

Plain paper plate • Scissors • Popsicle stick • Tacky glue • Paint • Markers • Construction paper • Chenille stems (optional)

DIRECTIONS

1 Cut two eye holes in a plain paper plate. Be sure to make them big enough so you can see clearly through them.

Here's A Tip

Try looking through the eye holes before decorating the mask. If they're too small, cut them bigger. You'll want to see clearly, so you can peek at your audience!

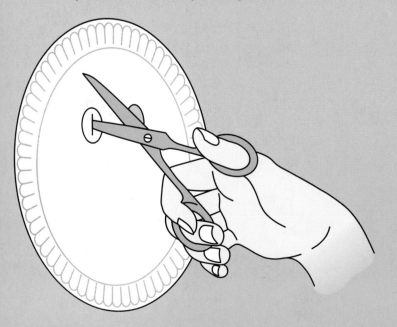

2 Turn the plate over and glue a popsicle stick to the back, near the bottom.

This will be the mask handle.

Let the glue dry completely.

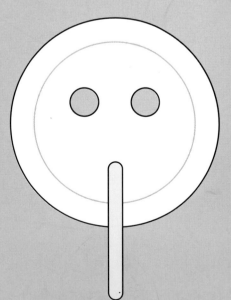

3 On the front, decorate the mask with paint, markers, or glued-on construction paper features.

Or, make a cat mask...

Paint or draw a nose, mouth, tongue, and fur markings. Then glue on construction paper ears and chenille stem pieces for whiskers. Let the glue dry *completely* before using the mask.

15

SOCK PUPPETS

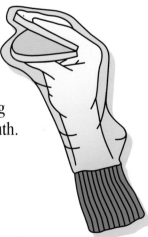

SUPPLIES

Lid from a small plastic container • Scissors • Masking tape • One clean, old sock • Tacky or fabric glue • Felt or fabric scraps • Markers

DIRECTIONS

1 Cut the lid in half. Place one half on top of the other so that the flat surfaces are together and the raised edges point out. Tape the two pieces together along the cut edge to make a hinge.

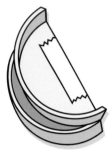

2 Push the hinged lid into the toe of the sock, with the round edge towards the toe. This will be the puppet's mouth.

If the lid is too big, use scissors to trim it down, just a bit at a time, until it fits in the sock.

3 Take the plastic lid back out of the sock and open it to spread glue on both halves.

Then fold the two halves together again, so the glued surfaces meet, and push the lid back into the sock, with the round edge towards the toe.

4 Lay the sock flat, with the heel facing up and the toe in front of you. With one hand on either side, feel the plastic lid through the toe of the sock. Open the hinged lid and push the end of the sock toe into the center of the open "mouth." Press the sock into the glue, then let it dry.

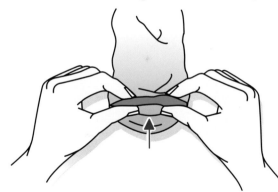

5 Now put your hand into the sock, with your fingers in the top part of the head and your thumb in the bottom part. Practice opening and closing the puppet's mouth.

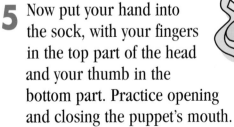

16

6 You're ready for the fun part–decorating! Make a snake.

From felt or fabric scraps, cut out eyes, nostrils, and a forked tongue. Glue each shape to the sock, then leave the puppet for a few minutes to let the glue dry completely.

You can also use markers to add details.

Here's A Tip

Sometimes, the glue used for the decorating pieces may soak through the sock and stick to the plastic lid inside. No problem. When the glue is completely dry, put your hand in the puppet and gently lift the sock away from the lid.

Or, try a lion puppet...

You can make a lion's mane with felt.

Cut a rectangle of felt the same width as the sock. Make a line of cuts along one edge of the felt, but don't cut all the way to the other edge. With fabric glue, attach the felt mane to the sock with the cut strips falling towards the toe of the sock. Only put glue along the uncut edge of the felt rectangle.

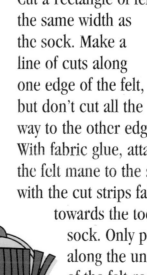

Now turn the sock over and do the same thing on the other side. Let the glue dry before using the lion puppet.

17

POPSICLE STICK

SUPPLIES

Old coloring book, magazine, or catalog • Crayons • Scissors • Popsicle stick • Craft glue • Family photos (optional) • Construction paper and a small paper cup (optional)

DIRECTIONS

1 Choose a character in a coloring book or an old magazine–one that's about the size of your hand. Color it and cut it out.

Don't cut from books that you want to save.

2 Spread glue on one end of a popsicle stick, just on the front.

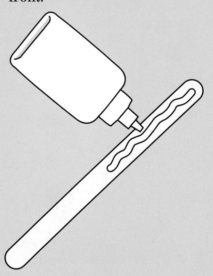

3 Lay the cutout picture on top of the glue and press gently. Let the glue dry for a few minutes before using the puppet.

Here's A Tip
Don't worry if you have too much glue and it shows along the edge of the popsicle stick. Most craft glues dry clear, so just wipe off any big blobs and let the rest dry.

PUPPETS

For a growing flower, try this...

Color and cut out a construction paper flower, then glue it to a popsicle stick. Add a pompom or sparkles if you like, then let the glue dry.

Use the end of your scissors to make a cut in the bottom of a small paper cup–just big enough to fit a popsicle stick through. Push the popsicle stick flower down through the inside of the cup, so that the stick shows out the bottom.

When you pull the popsicle stick down, the flower is hidden in the cup. Slowly push the stick up into the cup and your flower appears to be growing taller.

You can make a sun puppet too, to help the flower grow.

Or, try this...

If you have extra prints of family photographs, you can make mum, dad, brother, or sister puppets and perform a play about a special day with your family. Don't forget to make a puppet of yourself!
Cut out each figure and glue it to a popsicle stick. Let it dry for a few minutes.

19

TURNABLE TUBE HEADS

These puppets are designed to turn so that you can change their faces, hats, or outfits.
You can make one side happy and one side sad, or try mixing animal bodies with human faces.
Think of something outrageous to surprise your audience.
The sillier the better with these Tube Heads.

SUPPLIES

Two empty toilet roll tubes • Scissors • Construction paper • Pencil • Ruler • Craft glue
• Markers • Decorations–sparkles, pompoms, feathers (optional)

DIRECTIONS

1 Cut one toilet tube in three pieces. Make the first cut in the middle of the tube, then cut one part in half again. You'll have to squash the tube a bit to cut it, so open each piece out again after it's cut.

If the tube unwinds, glue it together again and hold it in place for a minute, until the glue dries.

The big part will be the body. The other two parts will form the face and hair.

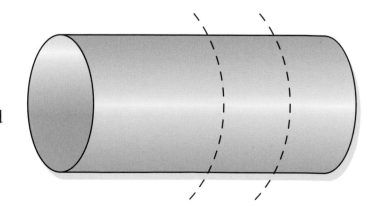

2 Choose different colors of construction paper for the hair, face, and body, and then glue paper around each tube section.

To cover each section, cut a strip of construction paper the same width as the tube. To find the cut line on the paper, lay the tube down on its side at the edge of the paper and make a pencil mark at the top and bottom edges. Using a ruler, draw a line joining the two marks, and cut along the line.

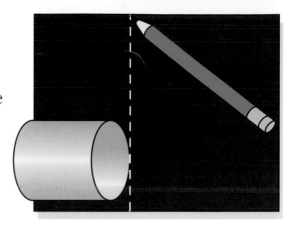

Apply glue all around the edges of the paper strip. Then wrap the paper around the tube. The easiest way is to lay the glued paper strip flat on the table, and roll the tube over it, sticking the paper on as you go.

Cover the three tube sections this way, using different colored paper for each.

Here's A Tip
Sometimes the edge of the construction paper won't stick to the tube. Just add a bit more glue and smooth the edge down with your finger. Don't worry about getting glue on your hands; it rubs off easily.

3 To make the base for the turning puppet, gently flatten the other toilet tube and fold it along the middle, lengthwise.

Carefully push this squashed toilet tube through the inside of each of the three paper-covered tube sections.

Start with the body section at the bottom, then the face, and then the hair section on top.

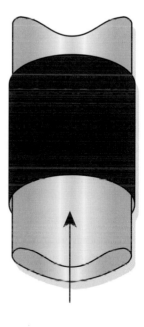

21

4 When all three pieces are on, poke your finger inside the flattened toilet tube in the middle, and open it out again as far as it will go.

It won't open out completely; there will still be a small crumple, but that's all right.

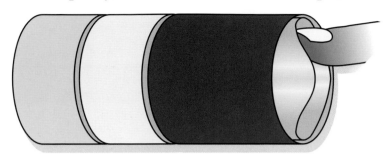

Try turning the Tube Head and think about what kind of face you want to give it. You can make a different face for each side. Maybe one side will be a lady and one side a man. Or how about Red Riding Hood's granny on one side and the big bad wolf on the other side? Anything goes!

5 Decorate the puppet with glued-on features or use markers to draw eyes, nose, and mouth.

NOTE   To make three-dimensional ears, see page 10.

For curly hair, make a line of cuts in a small piece of paper, but don't cut all the way to the bottom. Curl the cut ends by wrapping them around a pencil or your finger, then glue the paper curls onto the tube puppet.

Add a bow tie and buttons.

These puppets look best with silly faces and lots of bright colors.

Or, try a bird...

For a bird's beak, cut a small piece of construction paper like this.

Fold under the two tabs along the dotted lines, then fold the beak in half along the center dotted line. Open it out again. Put glue on the tabs and press them gently onto the tube puppet, in position. It's a little tricky gluing things onto a round tube, so hold the beak in place for a minute, until the glue holds.

23

FINGER

SUPPLIES

Felt and fabric scraps • Pen • Scissors • Tacky or fabric glue • Yarn and trim scraps • Buttons • Markers or fabric paint

DIRECTIONS

1 Place your hand on a piece of felt with your fingers spread out. Use a pen to draw around your index finger.

Don't make the line too close to your finger.

2 Move your hand and draw a second line around the first line, about a finger width away.

Then draw a line straight across the bottom.

Check that the puppet shape is wide enough. The bottom should be about four finger widths wide.

3 Cut out the puppet shape, following the *outside* line. This piece will be the back of the puppet.

Now place this shape on top of another piece of felt and trace around it. Cut out this second piece of felt. It will be the front of the puppet.

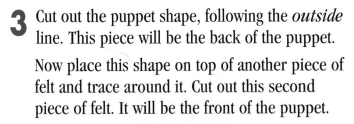

24

4 Put dots of glue around the curved edge of the back piece. Don't put any glue in the middle or across the bottom, where your finger will go in.

Then place the front piece on top of the back piece, to glue the puppet together.

Let the glue dry *completely*.

PUPPETS

5 Try on the finger puppet. It's ready for decorating!

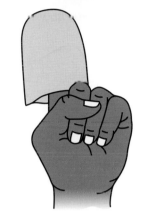

6 Cut out felt pieces for the face and hair and glue them on, or draw on features with markers or fabric paint.

Add lace or ribbon decorations.

Let the fabric glue dry completely before using the puppet.

Here's A Tip
To add small decorations (beads, buttons), drop a small dab of glue in position on the puppet. Then press the decoration down into the glue and remove your finger before the glue sticks to you.

Or, try this...
Use yarn for hair and add felt arms and legs. When you work the puppet, the legs will help to hide your hand.

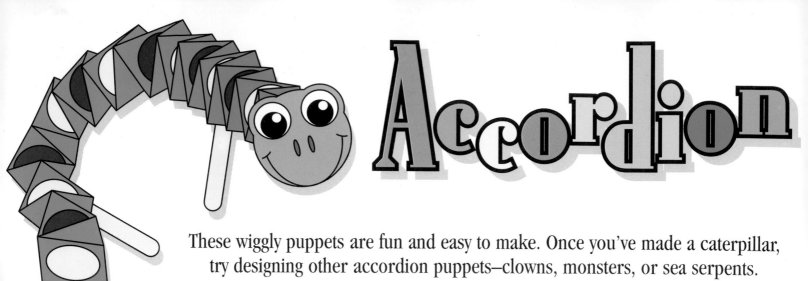

Accordion

These wiggly puppets are fun and easy to make. Once you've made a caterpillar, try designing other accordion puppets–clowns, monsters, or sea serpents.

SUPPLIES

Construction paper • Scissors • Craft glue • Chenille stem • Markers • Two popsicle sticks • Decorations–pom poms, stickers (optional)

DIRECTIONS

1 From a full sheet of construction paper, cut six strips about the same size.

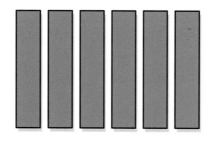

Here's A Tip

To divide a sheet of construction paper into equal size strips, try this trick.

Fold the paper in half along the long side. Then fold it in half again, two more times.

Mark the folds with a good crease, by pressing your finger down along each side of the folded paper.

When you unfold the paper, it will be divided into eight equal strips. To cut them out, cut along the fold lines with your scissors.

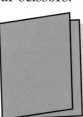  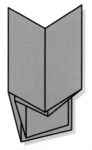 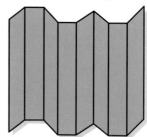

Caterpillar

2 Glue three strips together, end to end, to make one long strip.

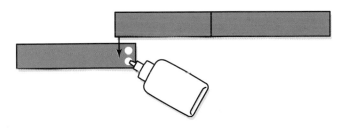

Do the same with another three strips of paper.

Once you have two long strips, you're ready to start the accordion puppet.

3

Glue the two long strips together at one end, to form an L shape.

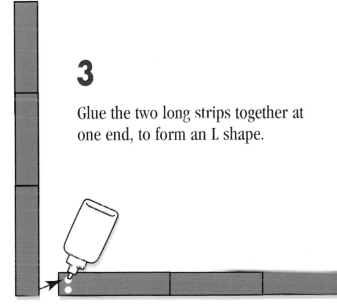

4 Starting with the bottom of the "L", fold this bottom strip across to make a backwards "L".

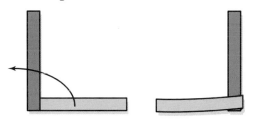

Then take the top of the "L" and fold it down.

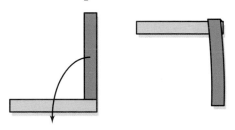

Continue crossing one piece over the other until all the paper is folded into an accordion shape.

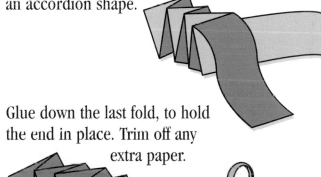

Glue down the last fold, to hold the end in place. Trim off any extra paper.

27

5 For the caterpillar's antennae, cut off half of a chenille stem and bend it in the middle.

Glue the bent chenille stem between two folds of paper near one end of the accordion puppet. Spread the glue around and press the folds of paper together. Let the glue dry completely.

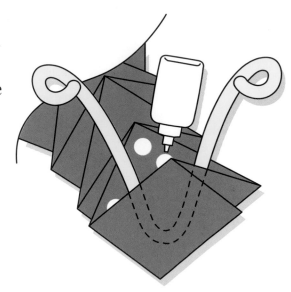

6

With another piece of construction paper, color and cut out a face for the caterpillar. Try giving it puffy cheeks so it looks like it's munching on a leaf.

Glue the face to the end with the antennae.

7 Glue a popsicle stick to the bottom, near each end of the caterpillar.

Insert each popsicle stick between two paper folds, add glue, and press the glued folds together.

Let the glue dry completely.

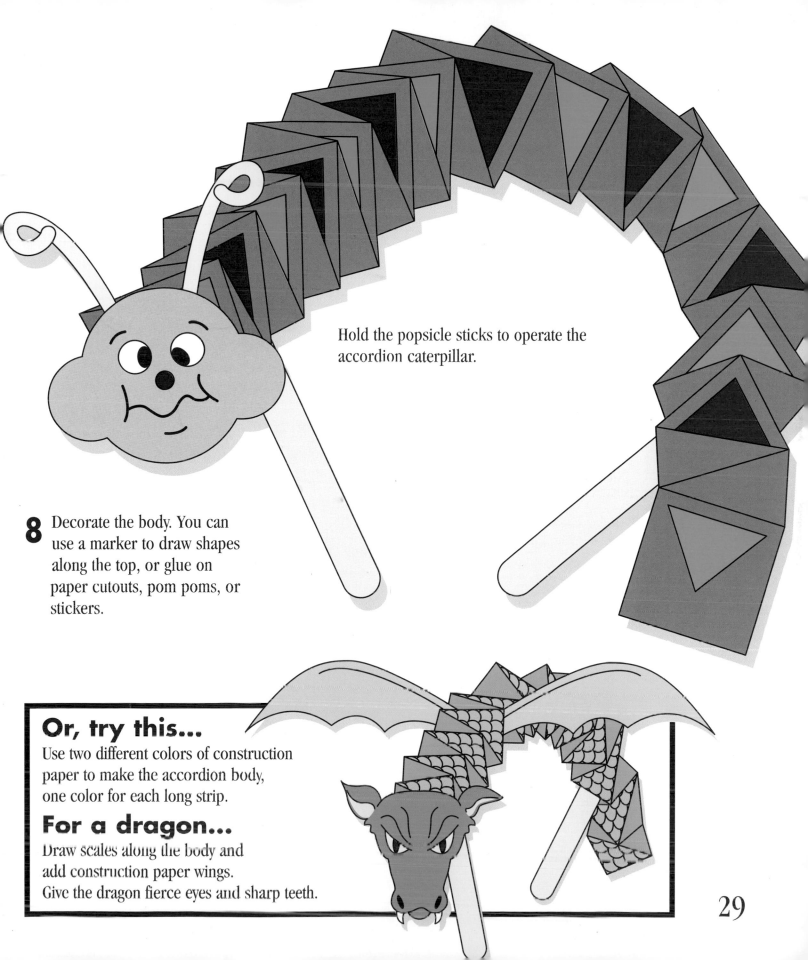

Hold the popsicle sticks to operate the accordion caterpillar.

8 Decorate the body. You can use a marker to draw shapes along the top, or glue on paper cutouts, pom poms, or stickers.

Or, try this...

Use two different colors of construction paper to make the accordion body, one color for each long strip.

For a dragon...

Draw scales along the body and add construction paper wings. Give the dragon fierce eyes and sharp teeth.

29

Spunky

SUPPLIES

Wooden spoon • Acrylic paints • Paint brush • Markers • Yarn • Tacky or fabric glue • Fabric squares • Chenille stem • Scissors • Decorations–felt and trim scraps, sequins, construction paper • Narrow plastic bottle (optional)

DIRECTIONS

1 Choose a skin tone to paint the top of a wooden spoon.

2 When the paint is dry, add a face with paints or markers.

3 For hair, glue braided yarn around the face and down the back of the spoon.

NOTE See braiding directions on page 9.

4 Cut a square of fabric about three times as big as your hand.

Bunch up one end of the fabric and wrap it around the neck of the spoon, with the opening at the back.

Twist a chenille stem around the neck to hold the fabric in place.

About one third of the way down the front of the fabric, cut two finger holes.

5 Try the puppet. Poke your thumb and index finger through the holes and hold the spoon with your other fingers.

30

Spoons

6 Add decorations to the puppet's costume. Glue on felt or paper cutouts, ribbon, sequins, beads, or artificial flowers.

Or, try this...

Paint a face on both sides of a wooden spoon. Try making one side awake and the other side sleeping. For hair, glue yarn only along the top and sides of the spoon. Glue fabric or paper around the spoon's handle, then add decorations.

Here's A Tip

Keep a narrow plastic bottle on your dresser or shelf. When you're not using your spoon puppet, put the handle in the bottle to hold the puppet upright.

SUPPLIES

Plain paper bag (with a flap bottom) • Scissors • Construction paper • Craft glue • Markers • Sparkles • Crushed eggshells (optional)

DIRECTIONS

1 Lay the paper bag flat on the table, with the flap at the top facing you.

For a bird puppet, cut two triangles from construction paper for the beak. Glue one triangle to the lower edge of the bag's flap, in the middle.

2 Lift the flap to glue on the other triangle, underneath the first triangle.

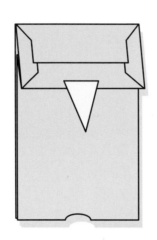

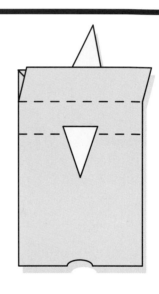

3 For a feathery effect, make a series of cuts along the bottom of the bag.

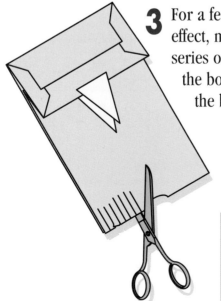

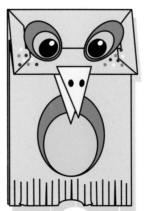

4 Use construction paper or markers to add eyes, nostrils, and patterns on the face and body.

For glitter, glue on sparkles or crushed eggshell bits.

Here's A Tip

To add the glitter, spread glue on the bird's cheeks. Then sprinkle the sparkles or eggshell bits over the wet glue. Let the glue dry, then gently shake off any extra pieces that aren't glued down.

BAG PUPPETS

5 Turn the bag over and glue on two construction paper tail feathers.

Or, make a turtle...
Glue a construction paper shell to the back of the paper bag.

On the front, glue on arms, legs, and body. Glue the head to the flap and the bottom part of the mouth to the bag, partly under the flap.

6 Cut out and glue on construction paper wings and head feathers.

To work the puppet, put your hand in and curl your fingers into the flap. Move your fingers to open and close the bird's mouth.

33

CARTON

SUPPLIES

Empty cereal box • Sharp point scissors • Pencils • Construction paper • Craft glue • Tape • Markers • Empty egg carton and tacky glue • Empty tissue box with top opening (optional) • Yarn (optional)

DIRECTIONS

1 Draw a line across the front and two sides of an empty cereal box, near the middle.

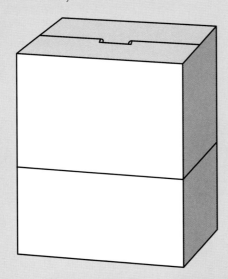

2 Use scissors to cut along the line. Be sure not to cut through the back of the box.

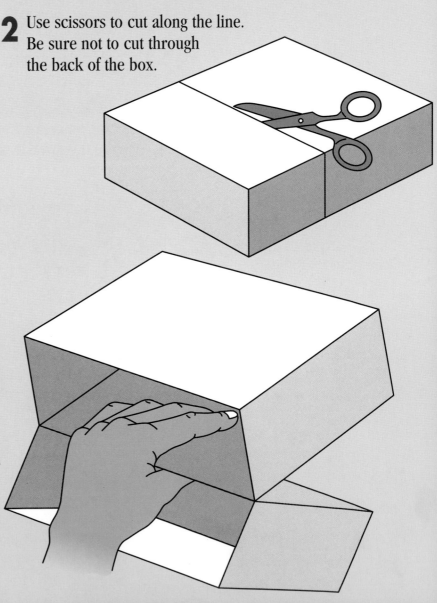

3 Fold along the uncut edge. This will be the hinge for the puppet's mouth.

If one half is bigger, make it the top of the puppet's head. Try to work the puppet with your fingers in the top and your thumb in the bottom opening.

34

CREATURES

4 To help work the puppet, make a strap for your fingers. Lay the cereal box flat, with the fold facing up. In the "top" or bigger part of the box, make two cut lines near the fold. The cuts should be about two finger widths apart and they should be big enough to fit your fingers.

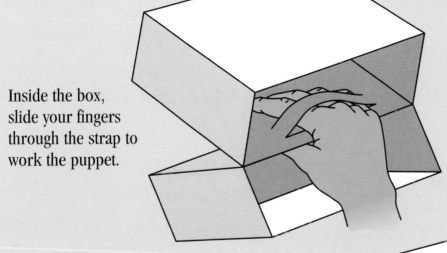

Inside the box, slide your fingers through the strap to work the puppet.

5 Take your fingers out and push two pencils in to lift the strap. This prevents the strap from being glued down when you glue paper on the outside of the box.

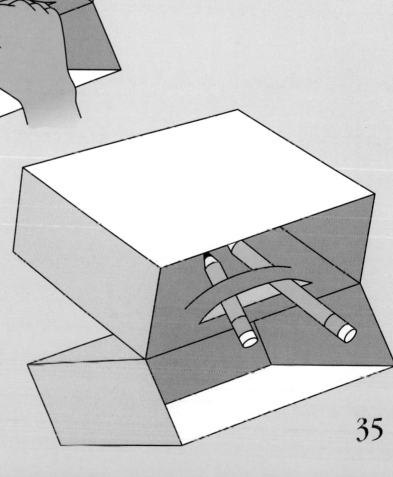

6 Cover the cereal box, one surface at a time, with construction paper.

Lay each side on a piece of paper and trace around it. Cut out the traced rectangle and glue it to the box.

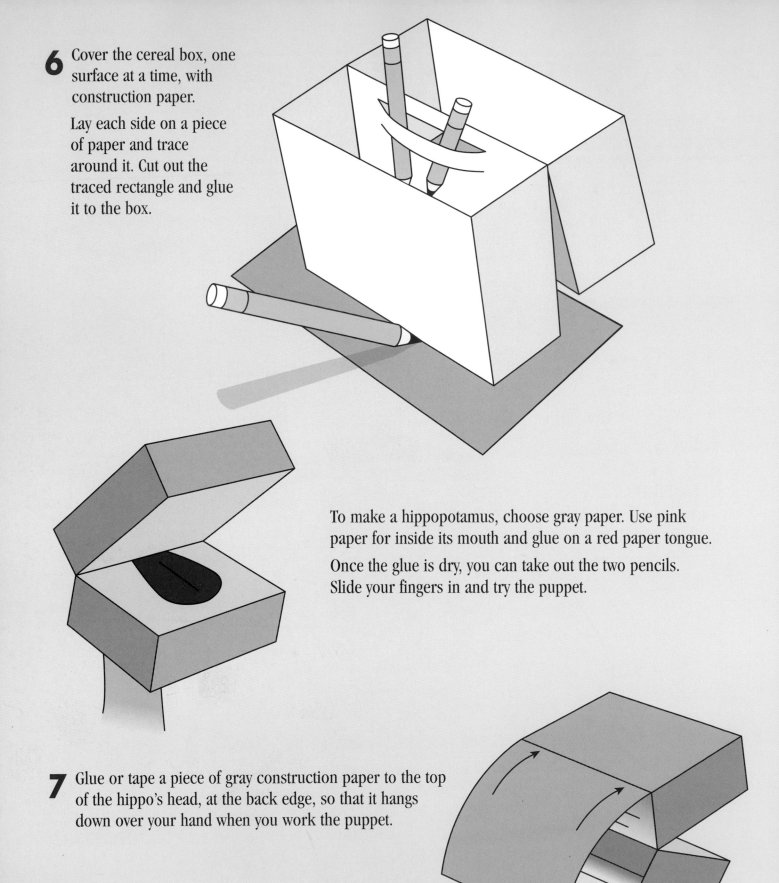

To make a hippopotamus, choose gray paper. Use pink paper for inside its mouth and glue on a red paper tongue.

Once the glue is dry, you can take out the two pencils. Slide your fingers in and try the puppet.

7 Glue or tape a piece of gray construction paper to the top of the hippo's head, at the back edge, so that it hangs down over your hand when you work the puppet.

8 Cut two ovals the same color as the head, and draw nostrils on them. Glue them on, sticking out beyond the sides of the box.

Glue on paper ears and teeth. Use bumps from a cardboard egg carton for the eyes.

Here's A Tip

For egg carton eyes, cut out two sections from the bottom of the carton. Put tacky glue all around the cut edge of each piece and press it onto the puppet's head. Hold it in place with one hand. With the other hand, push up from inside the puppet to squeeze the glue against the box. Let the glue dry *completely*.

Or, try this...

Use a large tissue box—the kind that opens on the top only– to make a Talking Head. Cut across the middle of the top and two sides. Fold along the bottom to form the mouth hinge and cut two slits where your fingers will go.

Cover the box with construction paper and decorate the talking head.

This character has a big nose, glasses, and curly yarn for hair.

CAN HEADS

SUPPLIES

Empty cardboard juice can • Construction paper • Pencil • Ruler • Scissors • Tacky or fabric glue • Fabric scraps • Felt • Markers or crayons • Decorations–pom poms, ribbon, buttons (optional)

DIRECTIONS

1 Choose skin colored construction paper to cover an empty juice can.

Lay the can down on its side at one edge of the paper and make a mark with a pencil at the top and bottom edges.

Using a ruler, draw a line joining the two marks, and cut along the line.

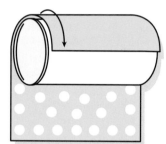

Put glue on one side of the trimmed paper, then wrap it around the can.

2 At the bottom (or *open* end) of the can, glue on a narrow strip of colored paper or fabric for a collar.

3 For hair, cut a rectangle of felt, wide enough to wrap all around the can.

Put glue along one long edge of the felt rectangle and glue this edge around the top of the can.

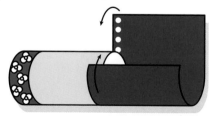

Once the glue is dry, use sharp scissors to make a series of cuts in the felt, all around. Cut up to the top of the can.

4 When you stand the can up, with the opening at the bottom, the cut felt will hang like hair.

Glue a circle of matching felt to the top of the can.

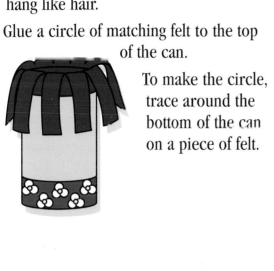

To make the circle, trace around the bottom of the can on a piece of felt.

5 Flip two or three strands of felt to the back to make room for the puppet's face. Draw or glue on eyes, nose, mouth, and ears.

NOTE   To make ears that stick out, see "Three Dimensional Ears" on page 10.

This puppet is wearing construction paper earrings.

Or, try this...

Glue on construction paper arms and make a hat for the can head character.

To make a construction paper cap, cut out a brim shape about one and a half inches wide.

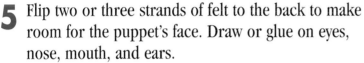

Glue the hat band around the top of the can and fold the brim up.

For the hat band, cut a strip of paper long enough to wrap all around the can. Glue the straight edge of the brim to the hat band.

39

Fabric

SUPPLIES

Felt squares • Pen • Scissors • Tacky or fabric glue • Felt scraps • Markers • Decorations–feathers, yarn, buttons, lace (optional) • Chenille stem (optional)

DIRECTIONS

1 On a piece of skin-colored felt, draw a puppet shape bigger than your hand.

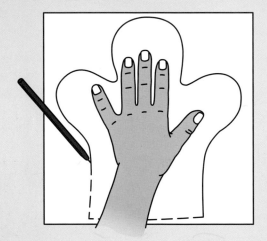

2 Cut out the puppet shape and lay it on top of another piece of felt. Trace around the shape, then cut out the second piece.

3 Spread a line of fabric glue around the edge of one of the felt pieces. Don't put glue along the bottom, where your hand goes in.

Then lay the second piece on top of the first, pressing the two together along the glue line.

4 Let the glue dry *completely* before trying on the puppet. You're ready to decorate.

Puppets

5 Cut out and glue on felt shapes for the face, hair, and clothes, or draw on details with markers.

For a pirate, glue on a felt eyepatch and a hat with a feather.

Or, make a kangaroo...

Cut out and glue on felt shapes for a kangaroo's head, pouch, and tail. Then cut out a felt baby to fit in the pouch.

Here's A Tip

Use a chenille stem to make the puppet hold small objects. First wrap one end of the chenille stem around something small, like a toy sword. Then, with one hand in the puppet, wrap the other end of the chenille stem tight around one of the puppet's hands.

41

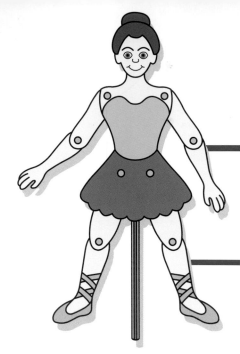

Jumping

Choose any character for a jumping puppet.
Follow the directions for a jumping gymnast,
then try an animal or even an insect.

DIRECTIONS

1 Draw all the puppet pieces on a piece of lightweight cardboard.
For the gymnast, the head and body are one piece. The arms
and legs should be drawn as eight separate pieces.

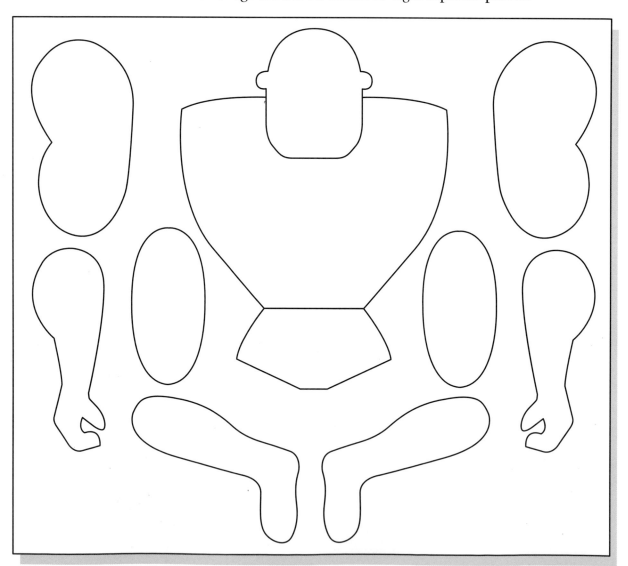

Gymnast

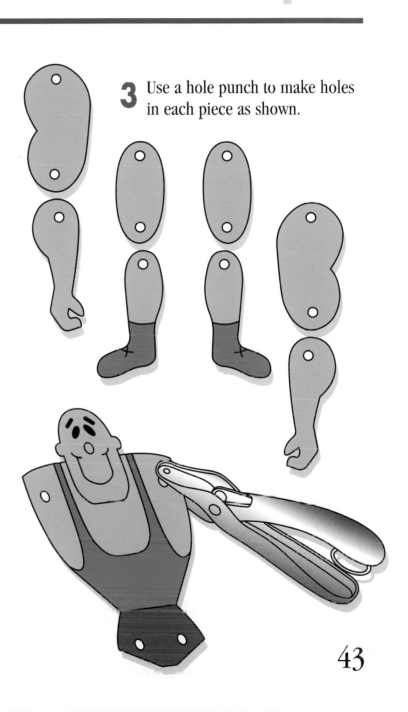

SUPPLIES

Lightweight cardboard (flattened cereal box or bristol board) • Pencil • Scissors • Construction paper • Craft glue • Markers • Hole punch • Eight brass fasteners • Straw • Tapc • Yarn

2 Cut out all the puppet pieces, then decorate cach one with markers or glued-on construction paper.

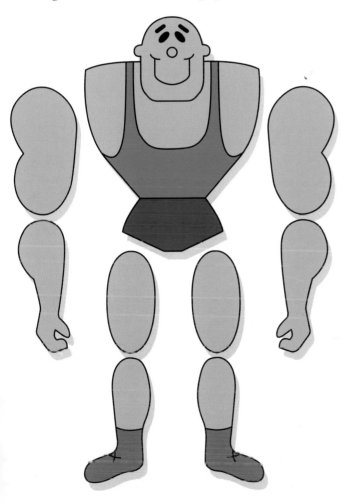

3 Use a hole punch to make holes in each piece as shown.

43

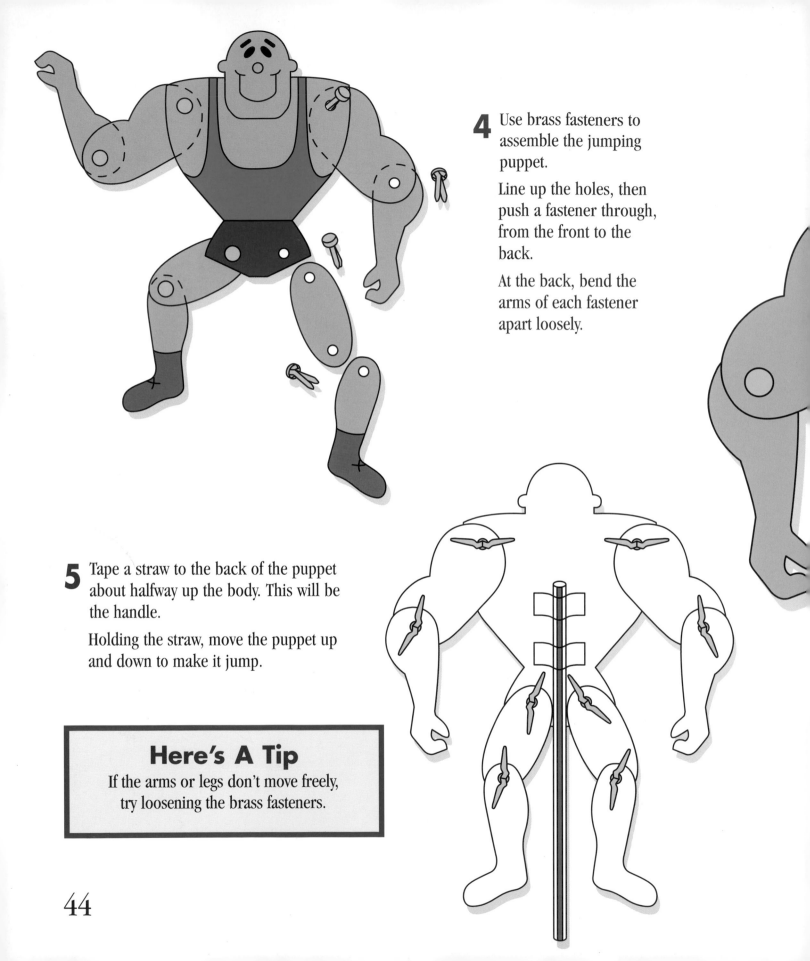

4 Use brass fasteners to assemble the jumping puppet.

Line up the holes, then push a fastener through, from the front to the back.

At the back, bend the arms of each fastener apart loosely.

5 Tape a straw to the back of the puppet about halfway up the body. This will be the handle.

Holding the straw, move the puppet up and down to make it jump.

Here's A Tip

If the arms or legs don't move freely, try loosening the brass fasteners.

44

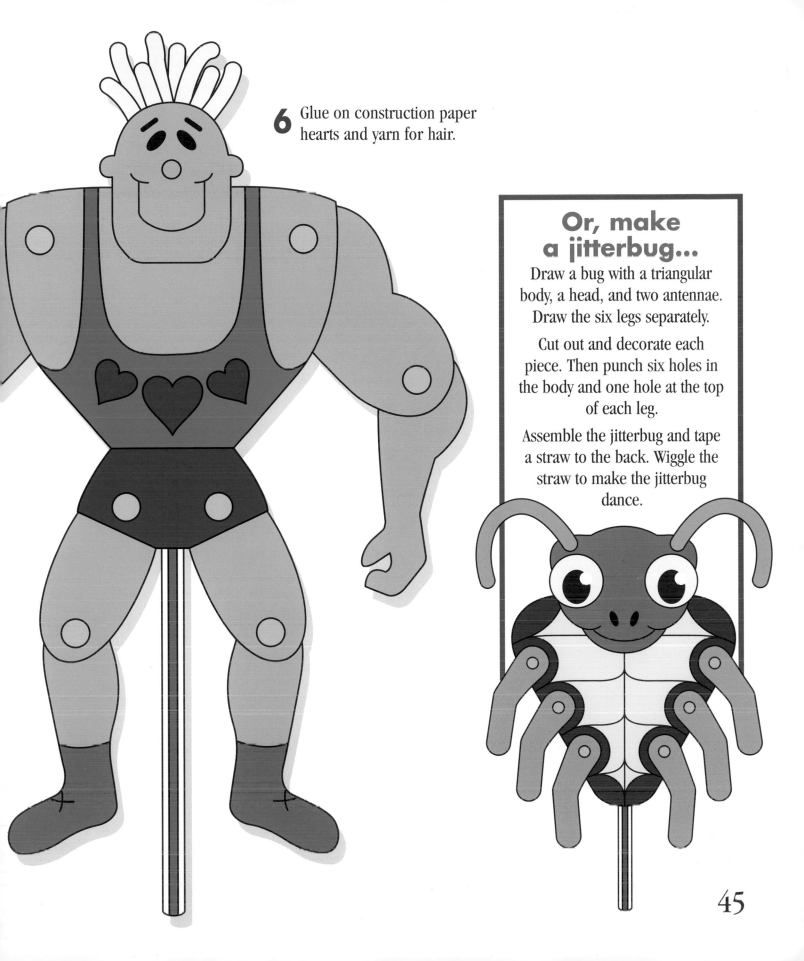

6 Glue on construction paper hearts and yarn for hair.

Or, make a jitterbug...

Draw a bug with a triangular body, a head, and two antennae. Draw the six legs separately.

Cut out and decorate each piece. Then punch six holes in the body and one hole at the top of each leg.

Assemble the jitterbug and tape a straw to the back. Wiggle the straw to make the jitterbug dance.

Dancing

SUPPLIES

Paper plate • Pencil • Scissors • Construction paper • Craft glue • Markers or crayons

DIRECTIONS

1 Draw two small circles near the bottom of a paper plate and cut them out.

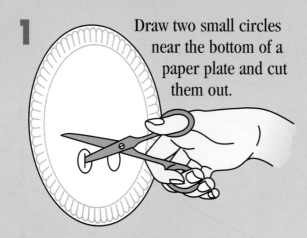

Check to see if you can fit two fingers through the holes. If not, cut the circles a bit bigger. Wiggle these two fingers in the holes, to make the paper plate dance.

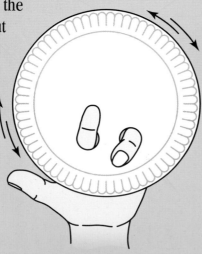

2 For a dancing dandelion, cut out small squares of yellow construction paper. Make a line of cuts along one edge of each square, but don't cut all the way to the other edge.

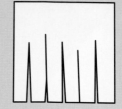

Make enough squares to cover the front of the plate.

Here's A Tip

To cut out lots of squares at one time, cut construction paper into strips. Lay the strips on top of each other, and make a line of cuts along one long edge, cutting through all layers at once. Remember not to cut all the way to the other edge. Then, cut the strips into squares.

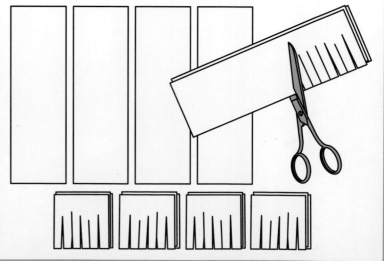

Paper Plates

3 Curl the ends around a pencil.

4 One at a time, put glue on the uncut edge of each square and glue it to the paper plate. Start by gluing squares around the rim.

Then cover the entire front of the plate. The squares can overlap and curl in different directions.

Don't put glue over the finger holes.

Glue on construction paper eyes and a mouth. Then, practice making your dandelion dance in the wind.

Or, make a bug...

Make the finger holes near the top of the plate, for the eyes. Cut out and glue on construction paper legs.

Insects come in every imaginable color and pattern, so have fun decorating this character! Add nostrils, a mouth, and patterns around the eye holes.

To give your insect crazy bug-out eyes, tape two small paper circles to the tips of the fingers that will work the puppet.

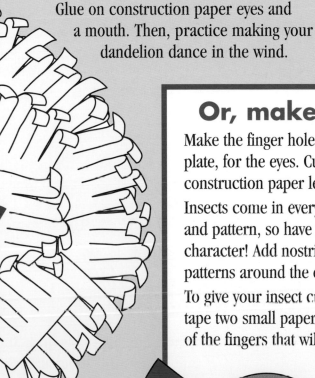

Tube Sock

SUPPLIES

One discarded tube sock • Four paper towels • Elastic band • Scissors • Felt scraps • Tacky or fabric glue • Markers • Yarn • Decorations–chenille stem, pom poms, ribbon (optional)

DIRECTIONS

1 Crumple four paper towels loosely into a ball and stuff the ball into the toe of a tube sock.

2 Wind an elastic band around the sock just below the ball, to form the puppet's neck.

3 Try on the puppet. Push your index finger into the head and your thumb and middle finger through the holes.

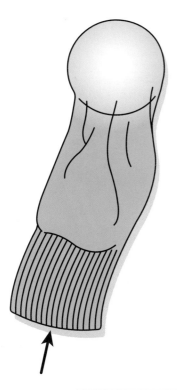

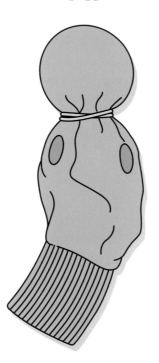

Then cut a finger hole in each side of the sock, about an inch below the elastic band.

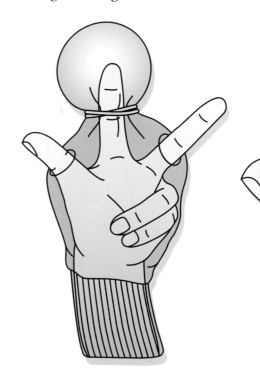

Here's A Tip

This puppet can hold small objects. With your hand in the puppet, squeeze your thumb and finger together to hold a pencil or other small prop.

48

People

4 For crazy hair, glue on different colors of yarn. Add felt cutouts for the face and use markers to add details.

Glue on ribbon decorations for the body.

Let the glue dry before using the puppet.

Or, try this...

Make eye glasses for the puppet. Near the middle of a chenille stem, make two loops by bending the stem around a finger.

Then twist the ends of the chenille stem together to form a large ring.

Push this ring down onto the puppet's head and position the loops over the eyes.

49

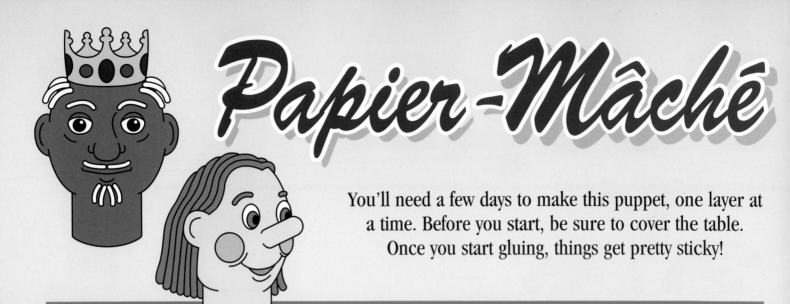

Papier-Mâché

You'll need a few days to make this puppet, one layer at a time. Before you start, be sure to cover the table. Once you start gluing, things get pretty sticky!

SUPPLIES

Old newspaper or sheet of plastic to cover the table • Empty toilet roll tube • Scissors • Small round balloon • Tape • Old newspaper • Bowl and spoon • Flour • Tempera or poster paints • Paint brush • Clear water-based acrylic urethane or shellac • Disposable foam brush • Felt squares • Tacky or fabric glue • Craft glue and salt (optional)

DIRECTIONS

1 Cut a piece off the end of an empty toilet tube for the puppet's neck.

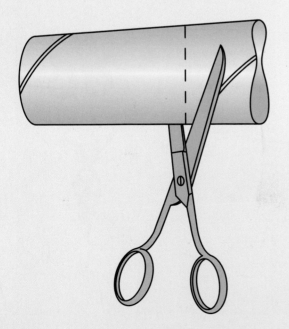

2 Blow up a round balloon to the size you want the puppet's head and tie off the end.

3 Gently push the balloon into the toilet tube neck and tape it in place. Use three or four pieces of tape, so that the balloon is secured all around the tube.

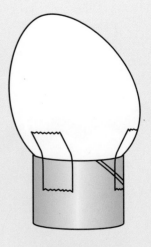

Puppets

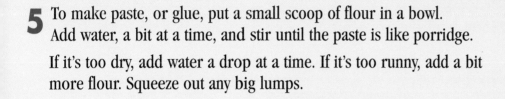

4 Tear a sheet of newspaper into thin strips. Tear along the grain, or down the long side of the paper. Then rip the strips in half and place them in a pile on one side of the work surface.

You're ready to start gluing.

5 To make paste, or glue, put a small scoop of flour in a bowl. Add water, a bit at a time, and stir until the paste is like porridge.

If it's too dry, add water a drop at a time. If it's too runny, add a bit more flour. Squeeze out any big lumps.

6 Drop a newspaper strip into the bowl and cover it completely with paste.

Then slide the paper through your thumb and index finger to get rid of any big lumps of paste.

7 Wrap the wet paper strip around the balloon and smooth it down.

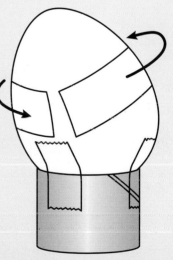

8 Using one paste-covered strip at a time, cover the whole head and neck. Spread glue on any dry spots and make sure none of the balloon is showing. Smooth out any bumps.

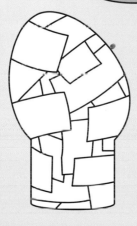

Here's A Tip
If the paper strips start sticking to you instead of the puppet head, stop and wash your hands before continuing.

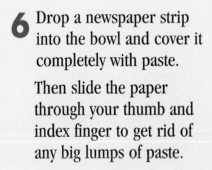

Find a safe place to leave your puppet overnight and put it on some newspaper to dry. Clean out the paste bowl right away. If it dries up, it will be hard to scrape the glue out.

9 When the first layer is dry, follow the same steps for a second layer. Make a fresh batch of paste and cover the whole head and neck again with paper.

With this layer, you can add shapes for the nose and ears.

Dip a strip of newspaper in paste and crumple it into a ball. Stick this ball in position for the nose. Then drape one or two pasted strips over the nose to hold it on. Smooth out any bumps and press the nose into the shape your want.

Do the same thing for each ear.

Leave the puppet head to dry overnight again.

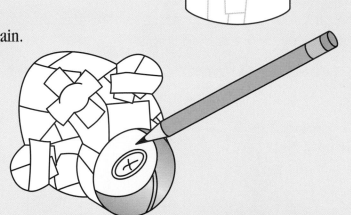

10 When the head is completely dry, use a sharp pencil to pop the balloon and pull out the balloon pieces.

11 Paint the head and neck a skin color. Once this is dry, you can paint on the face and hair.

Simple, bold features are best. You might want to paint the mouth open so it will look like it's talking.

When the paint is dry, you can add one coat of clear urethane or shellac to make the puppet head shiny. Use a disposable foam brush and be sure to work on a covered surface.

12 Make a body with felt pieces and fabric glue. Cut front and back pieces the same way you would for a fabric puppet, but without the top of the head.

NOTE   See fabric puppets on page 40.

Then glue the front piece to the front of the puppet's neck and the back piece to the back of the neck. Glue the sides together and let the glue dry completely.

Or, try this...

To add a rough texture to the finished puppet's head, spread craft glue over the dry paint wherever you want bumps. Then sprinkle salt over the wet glue.

Let the glue dry, then gently shake off any loose salt.

Glove Family

SUPPLIES

One discarded knit glove • Felt scraps • Scissors • Tacky or fabric glue • Yarn • Fabric paint • Lace and trim scraps

DIRECTIONS

1 Cut five felt circles for the glove family faces, big enough to cover the thumb and fingertips of an old glove.

2 Decorate each circle with felt cutouts for faces and ears. Glue on yarn or felt for hair and add details with fabric paint. For the baby's bonnet, glue lace trim around the head.

Here's A Tip

Before gluing the faces to the glove, plan where to place each one. The father might look best on the middle finger and the baby on the smallest finger.

3 Glue the faces to the glove thumb and fingertips, on the palm side.
Then add lace, felt, or ribbon decorations.

Or, try this...

Make a felt bee and four felt flowers.
Glue them to a glove to make a garden.

SPOOL JUMPERS

SUPPLIES

Three large straws • Lightweight string • Scissors • Medium to large size empty thread spool (to fit straw through center) • Skewer or knitting needle • Construction paper • Craft glue • Ruler • Markers • Decorations–sparkles, feathers, sequins, buttons, or beads • Fabric scraps and fabric glue (optional) • Lightweight cardboard and tacky glue (optional)

DIRECTIONS

1 Cut a piece of string about four times the length of one straw and drop the end of it through the center of the spool. Use a straw to help push it through if it sticks. Once the string is threaded through, tie a double knot tight around the outside of the spool, at one end of the string.

2 Take one straw and make sure it doesn't have any splits or cuts along the top edge. If it's not perfectly smooth, cut a bit off the top for a clean edge.

Push the straw through the center of the spool and drop the long end of the string through the top of the straw. If the string sticks on the way down, use a knitting needle or a meat skewer to push it through.

You now have the basic workings of the spool jumper puppet. Hold the straw and pull the string down to watch the spool jump up.

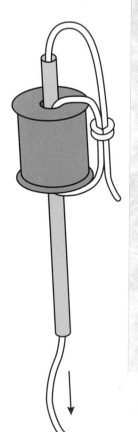

3 To keep the spool from falling off the bottom of the straw you'll have to tie a double or triple knot in the string, big enough that it won't fit through the straw. First, let the spool drop to the bottom of the straw. Hold the string just under the lower end of the straw. This is where you tie the knot.

Don't worry if the spool falls off the top of the straw. Just put it back on. Now you're ready to add a head, arms, and legs.

Here's A Tip
Make sure there's no label on the top or bottom of the thread spool that might cover any part of the hole. The opening should be smooth so that the straw can move up and down.

4 For the arms and legs, use two straws. Cut one straw in half, then cut each piece in half again to make four leg pieces. For the arms, start by cutting a bit off the end of one straw, so that the arms will be shorter than the legs, then cut this shorter straw in four equal pieces. Keep track of which four parts are for the arms.

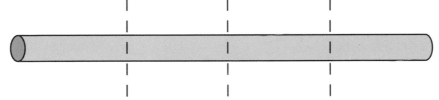

5 Decide what color clothes (fur, scales, feathers) you want, and choose paper or fabric to cover all eight straw pieces.

To cover each piece, follow these directions: Cut a piece of paper the length of the straw piece–big enough to cover it–and put a line of glue around the edges, and a few glue drops in between. Place the straw piece along one edge of the paper and push down into the glue. Carefully roll the paper strip around the straw. When you get to the end, a bit of glue will probably squeeze out along the edge of paper. Use your finger to spread this glue over the paper's edge and hold it for a few seconds to make sure the glue holds.

Cover each piece the same way.

6 Each arm and leg is made up of two covered straw pieces, threaded onto a piece of string.

Cut a piece of string about ten inches long. Tie a big knot in one end and thread on a bead or button. Then thread the string through one straw piece, a bead for the knee or elbow, and another straw piece.

Tie the completed arm or leg onto the spool near the top or bottom edge, in position. If you like, use a small dab of glue for each one, to hold the string in place on the spool.

Trim off any extra length of string, but don't cut too close to the knot.

Make as many arms and legs as you need.

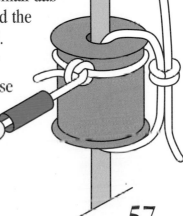

7 Using construction paper, draw a head with a long neck attached. Color it and cut it out.

Glue the neck to the spool right over the strings holding on the arms and legs.

To keep the head from falling forward, fold a small strip of paper and glue half to the back of the head and half to the top of the spool. Be sure not to glue over the hole in the center of the spool.

8 All that's left now is to cover the spool and decorate the body. Cut a rectangle of paper (or fabric) just big enough to fit around the middle of the spool. Before gluing it on, move the arms and legs out of the way, but leave the loose ends of string. These bits of string, and the extra long neck, will be covered when you glue on the last bit of paper for the body.

Glue this paper around the spool the same way you glued paper around the straws.

You're ready to decorate the spool jumper. You can add buttons down the front, sparkles all over, anything you want!

58

How about a jumping rock star?

You can cut a guitar shape out of cardboard or from two pieces of paper glued together for extra strength. Using tacky glue, glue the arms to the guitar, in position for playing.
Let the glue dry *completely*.

Now tune in to your favorite music and let the show begin!

Or, try this...

Maybe your puppet show needs a swooping prehistoric bird. You could design a pterodactyl by making the legs shorter and adding wings instead of arms. Cut the wings from one piece of construction paper, with space in between to glue the paper onto the spool body.

Attach the legs and head, then cover the body. Glue the wings on last.

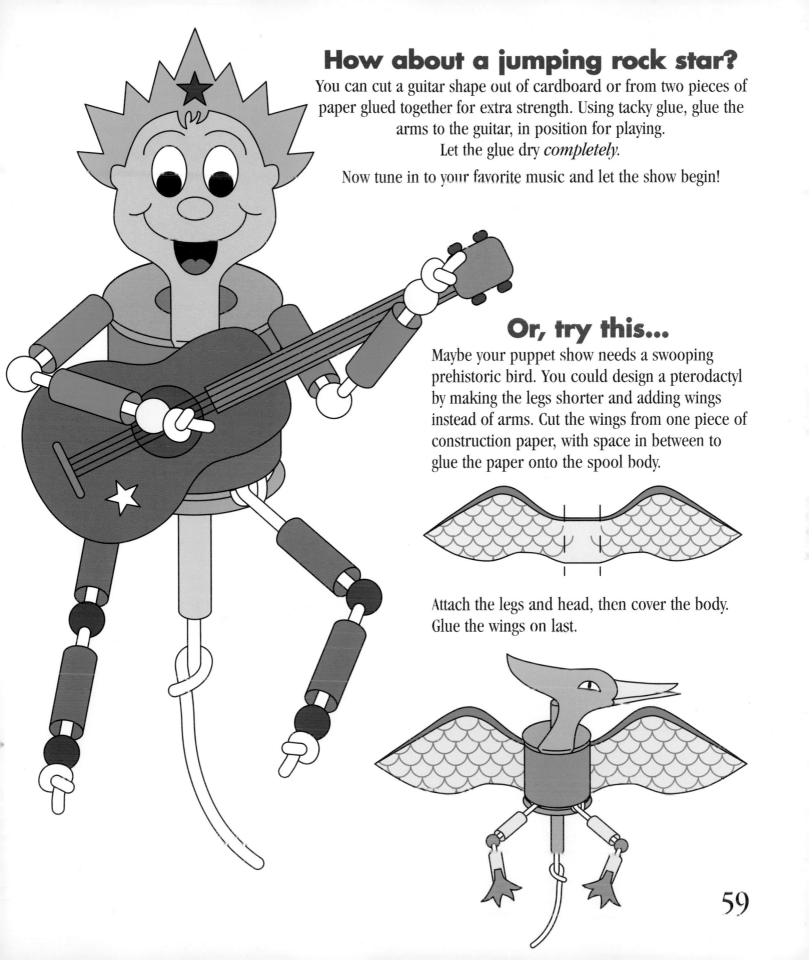

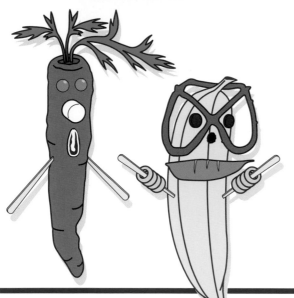

KITCHEN

These puppets are different from the others in this book. Because they're made of food, they will spoil quickly, but enjoy them for a day or two. Then, you can make a fresh one!

SUPPLIES

One washed carrot • Toothpicks • Scissors • Tacky glue • Uncooked macaroni noodles • Raisins, corn kernels, broccoli, cereal pieces, beans... • Uncooked rigatoni noodles • Potato (optional)

DIRECTIONS

1 Break three toothpicks in half and push the six pieces into a carrot, in a circle around the top.

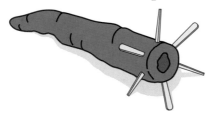

2 Put a small dab of glue on the end of each toothpick.

Then slide a macaroni piece on the end of each one, over the glue.

3 Find food decorations for the puppet's face. This carrot has raisins for eyes and a corn kernel nose.

Break additional toothpicks into small pieces and poke in one toothpick piece for each decoration. Then put a dab of glue on the raisin or corn and press it onto the end of the toothpick.

4 Attach the ears to the carrot the same way you attached the raisins and corn, with toothpick pieces and glue. These ears are broccoli.

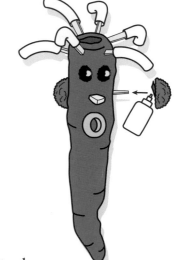

5 Add a mouth. This character has a glued-on cereal piece mouth. Yours might have a candy or a sunflower seed—whatever you find in your kitchen.

60

CREATIONS

6 Use rigatoni noodles for the arms. First poke a whole toothpick into each side of the carrot, angled up. Then put a dab of glue along the top side of each toothpick and slide a noodle onto each one. Let the glue dry completely.

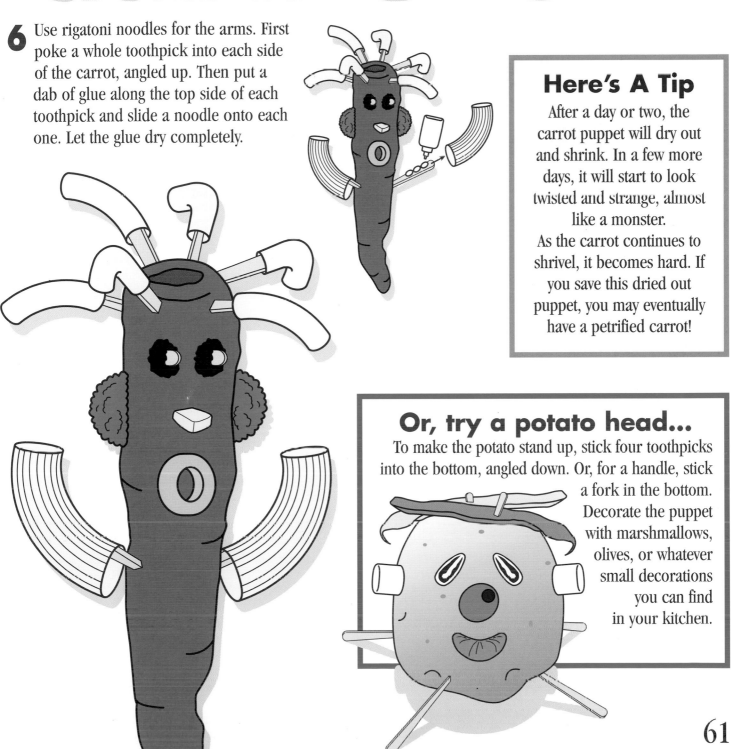

Here's A Tip

After a day or two, the carrot puppet will dry out and shrink. In a few more days, it will start to look twisted and strange, almost like a monster.

As the carrot continues to shrivel, it becomes hard. If you save this dried out puppet, you may eventually have a petrified carrot!

Or, try a potato head...

To make the potato stand up, stick four toothpicks into the bottom, angled down. Or, for a handle, stick a fork in the bottom. Decorate the puppet with marshmallows, olives, or whatever small decorations you can find in your kitchen.

SLEEPING GIANT

Surprise your audience with a puppet whose eyes open and close. Make a sleeping giant, then try a monster or a singing puppet with a movable mouth.

SUPPLIES

Empty paper towel tube • Construction paper • Pencil • Scissors • Craft glue • Tape • Popsicle stick • Markers • Decorations–buttons, ribbon, stickers (optional)

DIRECTIONS

1 Cover an empty paper towel tube with construction paper.

First, lay the tube down on its side at one edge of the paper and make a pencil mark at the top and bottom edges.

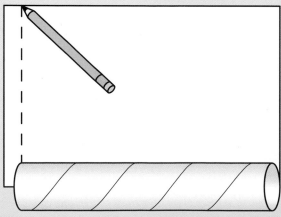

Using a ruler, draw a line joining the two marks and cut along the line. Then glue the trimmed paper around the cardboard tube. Press the edge down for a minute, until the glue sets.

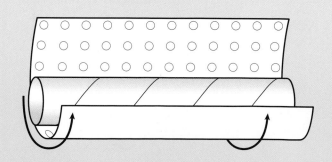

2 Cut a strip of the same colored paper, about two inches deep and wide enough to wrap around the tube.

Roll this paper band around the tube and tape the edge down. It should be just loose enough to slide up and down the tube.

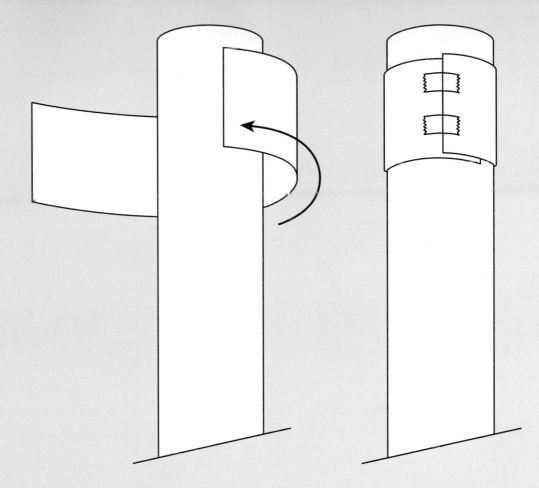

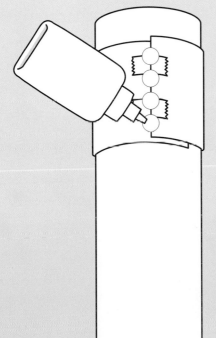

3 Put dots of glue along the seam of the paper band and press the top half of a popsicle stick into the glue.

When the glue is completely dry, use the popsicle stick handle to slide the band up and down.

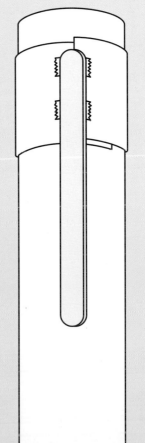

63

4 Push the paper band all the way up and use markers to draw a face on the tube.

The eyes should be just below the bottom of the movable band and should be wide open.

5 Slide the band down to just cover the open eyes. Then draw eyebrows and closed eyelids on the paper band.

6 With the band still down, so the eyes are closed, glue on paper ears. The top of each ear should be just below the movable band.

NOTE   To make three-dimensional ears, see page 10.

7 Draw or glue on hair, clothes, arms, and decorations.

NOTE   To make three-dimensional arms, see page 10.

Here's A Tip

Be sure the open eyes are completely covered before gluing on the ears.

Now SHHHH, or you'll wake the giant!

Or, try this...

To make a monster with a mouth that opens and closes, position the movable band near the middle of the tube, over the mouth.

First, draw a face on a covered tube with the mouth open wide and sharp teeth. Then tape a strip of paper around the tube and move it up to cover the open mouth. Draw a closed mouth on the paper band.

To open and close the mouth, move the band down and up. Glue paper arms to the movable band.

DRINKING BOX ROBOT

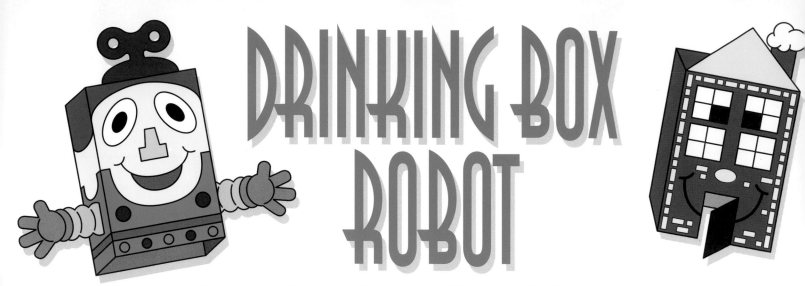

You can make unusual puppets with empty drinking boxes.
Follow the directions for a robot, then try a train or a talking
building. What other box-shaped characters can you think of?

SUPPLIES

Empty drinking box (or single serving cereal box) • Scissors • Aluminum foil • Tacky glue
• Construction paper • Decorations–stickers, beads, pop tab, buttons, cotton ball (optional)

DIRECTIONS

1 Lift the two V-shaped flaps at the top of the drinking box and cut them off.

2 Cut along the top seam, then cut the top of the box off completely. This is where you'll insert your hand.

Rinse the box out and let it dry.

3 To cover the drinking box, cut a piece of aluminum foil about two inches longer than the box and wide enough to wrap around it. Put glue on all four sides of the box and lay it on the middle of the foil.

Here's A Tip

Aluminum foil is hard to stick. Be sure to use *tacky* glue and let the glue dry completely.

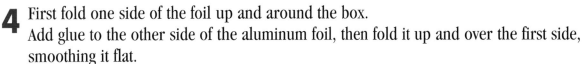

4 First fold one side of the foil up and around the box.
Add glue to the other side of the aluminum foil, then fold it up and over the first side, smoothing it flat.

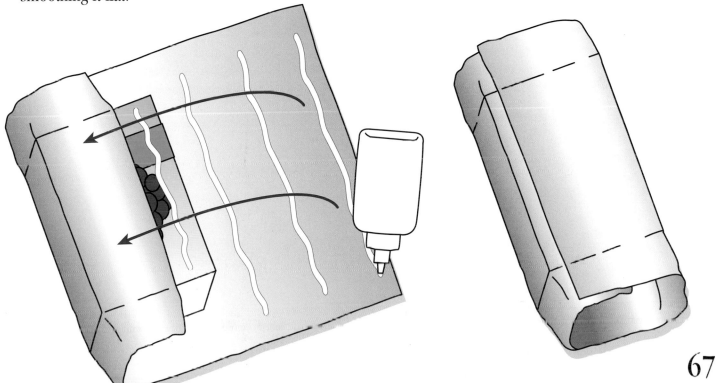

67

5 At the open end, fold the loose aluminum foil into the box.

At the closed end, glue the loose foil down, one side at a time, by pressing each side flat against the end of the box.

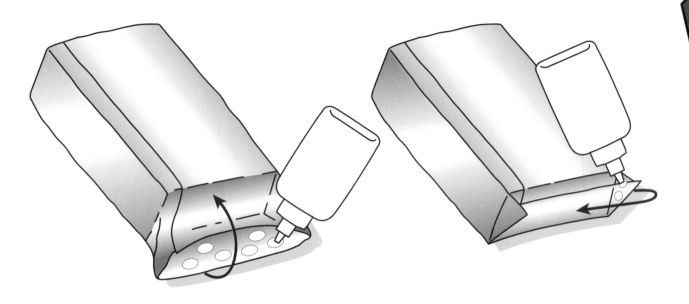

6 Turn the box so the opening is at the bottom.

Then decorate the robot with glued-on construction paper cutouts.

7 Glue on stickers, beads for eyes, a pop tab nose, buttons for control knobs, and accordion paper arms.

NOTE   To make accordion shapes for the arms, see page 27.

To work the puppet, put your hand in the opening at the bottom.

Or, try this...

To make a steam engine, cut away one narrow side of an empty drinking box and rinse the inside. Cover the box with construction paper and decorate with glued-on paper cutouts. To make smoke, glue a cotton ball to the smoke stack.

69

Marionettes

Marionettes are string puppets. Pull on the strings attached to the head and arms to make the puppet move. With your own marionette, you can stage a puppet performance wherever you go!

SUPPLIES

Two empty cardboard juice cans • Scissors • Two plastic single serving snack containers • Construction paper • Pencil • Ruler • Tacky glue • Hole punch • Pen or compass • Markers • Decorations–sequins, yarn, ribbon • Fabric scraps • Stapler • String • Empty paper towel tube • Felt scraps • Six toilet rolls (optional)

DIRECTIONS

1 Use two empty juice cans for the marionette's head and body.

Cut one in half and the other near the metal bottom. Discard the two bottom pieces.

2 The puppet is made of four parts–two juice can parts for the head and body, and two empty plastic snack containers for the feet.

Cover these four parts with construction paper.

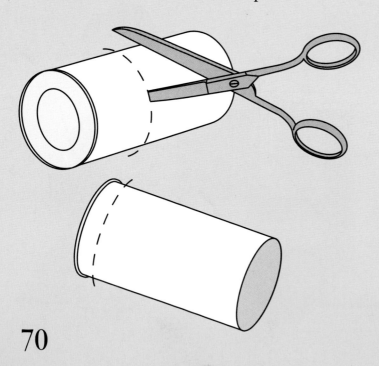

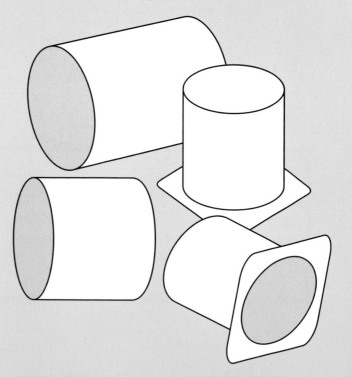

70

3 To cover each part, lay it down on its side at one edge of the construction paper and make a mark with a pencil at the top and bottom edges. Using a ruler, draw a line joining the two marks and cut along the line.

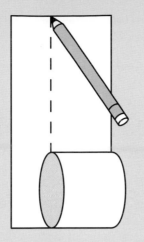

Put glue on one side of the trimmed paper, then wrap it around the puppet part.

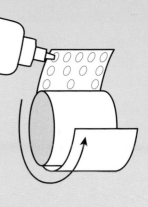

4 Punch holes in the body, head, and two feet.

Use a hole punch to make four holes in each juice can part—one at the top and one at the bottom, on each side.

Use a pen tip or the sharp point of a compass to punch a hole in the bottom of each snack container.

5 Decorate the four parts before assembling the marionette. Use glued-on construction paper cutouts or markers to give the puppet a face and to add details to the body and feet. Glue on sequins, yarn, or ribbon decorations.

NOTE   To make three-dimensional ears, see page 10.

For a skirt, cut strips of fabric and glue them around the puppet's waist.

6 Make two construction paper chains long enough for arms. Staple one arm to each side of the body, in position, and glue on paper hands.

NOTE   To make paper chains, see page 8.

71

7 Assemble the puppet with string.

Loop a piece of string through the lower hole in the head and the upper hole in the body on each side, and secure it with a double knot.

For the feet, cut two ten inch pieces of string and double knot each one through a hole at the lower edge of the body.

Push the loose ends of string through the holes in the snack containers, from the outside. Pull the string through from the inside and make a triple knot at the end of each piece, bigger than the holes in the snack containers.

8 Cut one twenty-four inch piece of string and two twenty-six inch pieces.

Push the shorter piece of string through the two holes in the top of the puppet's head and tie a triple knot. Then tie the loose end of the string around the middle of a paper towel tube.

Punch a hole in each arm and knot one twenty-six inch piece of string through each hole. Tie the loose end of each arm string around the paper towel tube.

Here's A Tip

If the marionette gets tangled, slide the two arm strings off the ends of the paper towel tube to untangle them. Then slide them back onto the tube, in position.

9 For hair, cut felt strips long enough to cover the top of the head. Put a line of glue around the top edge of the head and lay the felt strips across the opening, pressing them into the glue. Cross them over each other, to fill the empty space.

To work the marionette, pull up first on one side of the paper towel tube, then on the other.

Or, make a snake...

Decorate six toilet tubes with glued-on construction paper and markers. Punch a hole on each side of the head and knot a piece of string through each hole. Thread the two pieces of string through four more toilet tubes, then tie them through two holes punched in the last tube.

To attach the snake to the paper towel tube, punch two holes, one in its head and one near the middle. Tie a piece of string through each of these two holes and tie the loose ends to the paper towel tube.

73

Puppet Stages

Are you ready for a puppet show? You can use the furniture in your house as a stage. Hide behind a sofa or two chairs covered with a large towel.

For a larger stage, drape a tablecloth over the front of a table and hold it in place with heavy cans. Work your puppets from behind the table.

Or balance a broomstick across two chairs and drape a large towel, fastened with clothespins, over the stick.

For more detailed stages, follow the directions to cut and decorate cardboard cartons.

SUPPLIES

Large rectangular cardboard carton (available at grocery stores) • Heavy duty scissors • Construction paper • Craft glue • Markers • Utility knife and adult's help (optional)

DIRECTIONS

1 Use scissors to cut off the two long flaps from the top of a rectangular cardboard carton.

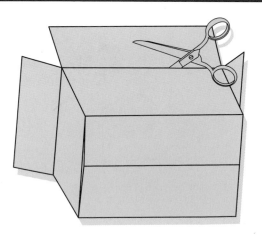

Here's A Tip
It's difficult to cut through heavy cardboard. You may want to ask an adult for help.

2 Turn the box upside down and draw a big window on the bottom of the box. This is the side the audience will see.

To cut out the window, first pierce the cardboard with the tip of the scissors, then cut along the line. Where there are two layers of cardboard, cut through one layer at a time.

3 Lay the box on its side, with the window facing forward and the two flaps at the sides.

Decorate the puppet stage with paint or glued-on construction paper cutouts. Be sure to cover any printed surfaces.

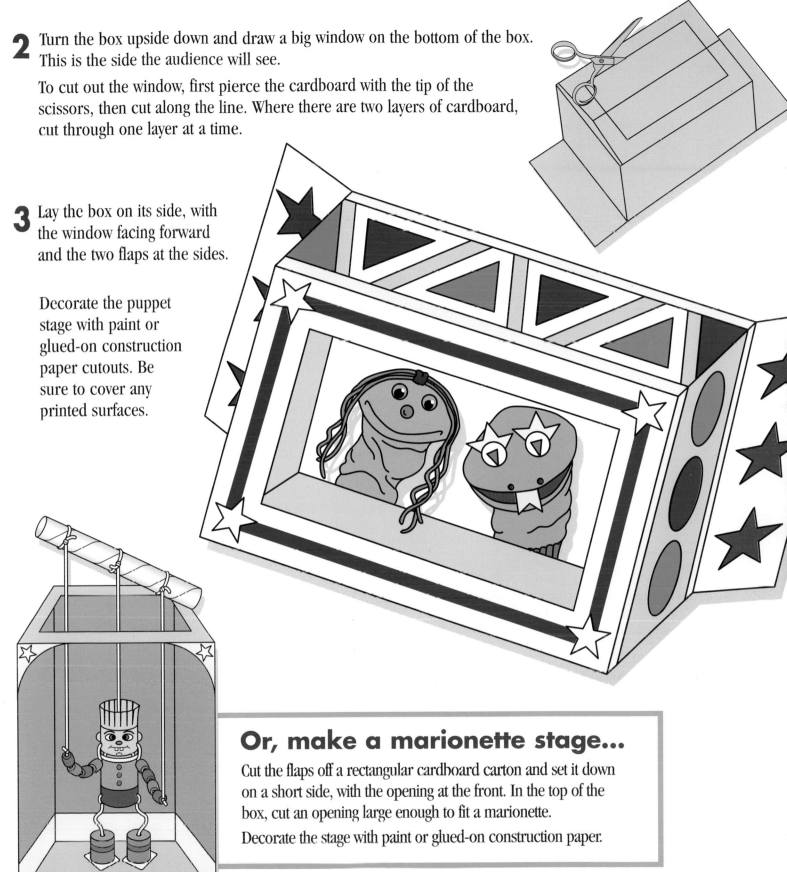

Or, make a marionette stage...

Cut the flaps off a rectangular cardboard carton and set it down on a short side, with the opening at the front. In the top of the box, cut an opening large enough to fit a marionette.

Decorate the stage with paint or glued-on construction paper.

PUPPET

Choose a story from a favorite book or make up your own puppet play. You can work with friends or stage a show on your own.

Before the show begins, practice moving your puppets. Make each puppet clap its hands, blow a kiss, wave hello, or bow to the audience. Exaggerated movements are best.

The puppet's face is often the most interesting part, so turn it to face the audience as much as possible. And, with more than one puppet, be sure to take turns. Only one puppet should talk or move at a time.

What kind of voice should each puppet have? Loud? Soft? Gruff? Practice different voices and remember to speak clearly, so the audience will understand.

To add sound effects, use musical instruments or experiment with things from around the house. Roll rice around a tin plate, tap a shoe on the floor, or let the air out of a balloon. What other sounds can you think of?

You can use a flashlight as a spotlight on your puppet stage. If it's bright enough, turn off the other lights in the room.

SHOWS

To make your puppet show more interesting, try drawing backdrops–pictures of things related to the story–and taping them to the back of the stage or to the wall behind you.

With a carton stage, you can add hanging props. Tape one end of a piece of thread to a paper cutout and then tape the other end to the inside top of the stage.

Paint a poster to announce your puppet show and make tickets for each member of the audience.

Then, enjoy your performance. You'll have fun bringing your puppets to life!

PUPPET SHOW

PUPPET SHOW
ADMIT ONE

PUPPET SHOW
ADMIT ONE

MORE IDEAS

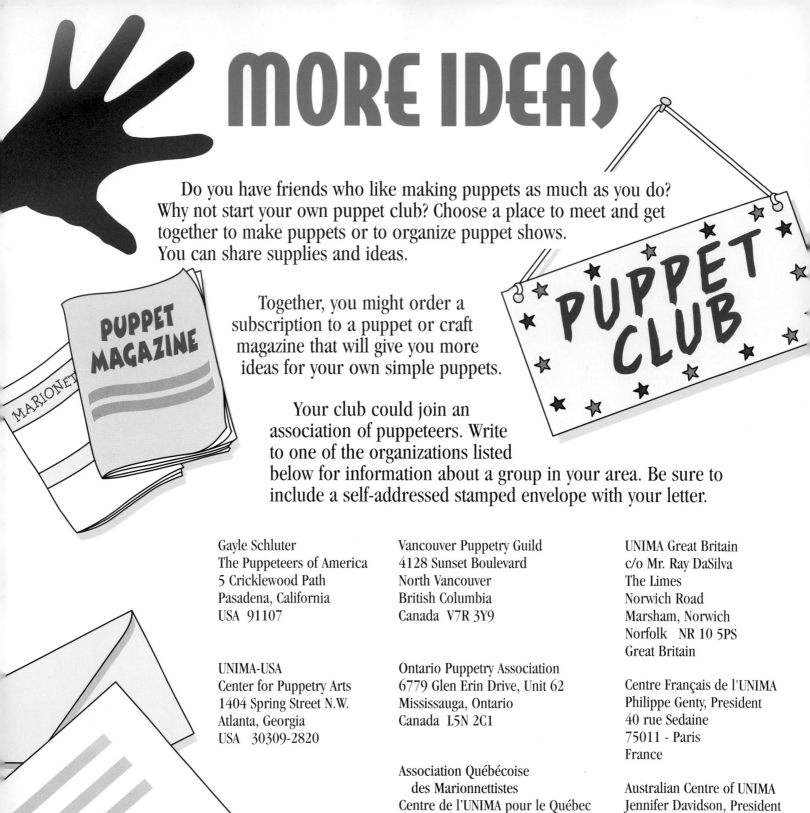

Do you have friends who like making puppets as much as you do? Why not start your own puppet club? Choose a place to meet and get together to make puppets or to organize puppet shows. You can share supplies and ideas.

Together, you might order a subscription to a puppet or craft magazine that will give you more ideas for your own simple puppets.

Your club could join an association of puppeteers. Write to one of the organizations listed below for information about a group in your area. Be sure to include a self-addressed stamped envelope with your letter.

Gayle Schluter
The Puppeteers of America
5 Cricklewood Path
Pasadena, California
USA 91107

UNIMA-USA
Center for Puppetry Arts
1404 Spring Street N.W.
Atlanta, Georgia
USA 30309-2820

Vancouver Puppetry Guild
4128 Sunset Boulevard
North Vancouver
British Columbia
Canada V7R 3Y9

Ontario Puppetry Association
6779 Glen Erin Drive, Unit 62
Mississauga, Ontario
Canada L5N 2C1

Association Québécoise
   des Marionnettistes
Centre de l'UNIMA pour le Québec
Case Postale 7
Succursale De Lorimier
Montréal, Québec
Canada H2H 2N6

UNIMA Great Britain
c/o Mr. Ray DaSilva
The Limes
Norwich Road
Marsham, Norwich
Norfolk   NR 10 5PS
Great Britain

Centre Français de l'UNIMA
Philippe Genty, President
40 rue Sedaine
75011 - Paris
France

Australian Centre of UNIMA
Jennifer Davidson, President
62 York Street
Sandy Bay
Tasmania 7005
Australia